199 FUN FAMILY ACTIVITIES

BARBOUR
PUBLISHING

© 2009 by Barbour Publishing, Inc.

Compiled and written by MariLee Parrish.

ISBN 978-1-60260-379-0

All rights reserved. No part of this publication may be reproduced or transmitted for commercial purposes, except for brief quotations in printed reviews, without written permission of the publisher.

Churches and other noncommercial interests may reproduce portions of this book without the express written permission of Barbour Publishing, provided that the text does not exceed 500 words and that the text is not material quoted from another publisher. When reproducing text from this book, include the following credit line: "From *199 Fun Family Activities*, published by Barbour Publishing, Inc. Used by permission."

Scripture quotations marked KJV are taken from the King James Version of the Bible.

Scripture quotations marked NIV are taken from the HOLY BIBLE, NEW INTERNATIONAL VERSION®. NIV®. Copyright © 1973, 1978, 1984 by International Bible Society. Used by permission of Zondervan. All rights reserved.

Scripture quotations marked NLT are taken from the *Holy Bible*, New Living Translation, copyright © 1996, 2004. Used by permission of Tyndale House Publishers, Inc. Wheaton, Illinois 60189, U.S.A. All rights reserved.

Scripture quotations marked MSG are from *THE MESSAGE*. Copyright © by Eugene H. Peterson 1993, 1994, 1995, 1996, 2000, 2001, 2002. Used by permission of NavPress Publishing Group.

Published by Barbour Publishing, Inc., P.O. Box 719, Uhrichsville, Ohio 44683, www.barbourbooks.com

Our mission is to publish and distribute inspirational products offering exceptional value and biblical encouragement to the masses.

Member of the
Evangelical Christian
Publishers Association

Printed in the United States of America.

Introduction

The home is a place to love and train up your children to know the Lord. . .and a place to have some wholesome fun! This book contains 199 activities for you to do together as a family. So whenever you hear "I'm bored!" you'll have a whole book of ideas to relieve those boredom blues.

I have come that they may have life,
and have it to the full.

JOHN 10:10 NIV

-Compliments Jar-

Everyone needs a little encouragement!
Spend time celebrating your family with this craft
activity that's sure to put a smile on every face.

Materials:
Large glass or plastic jar
Markers or puffy paint
Construction paper or felt
Family photos
Glue
Scissors

Using markers or paint, allow all family members to
write their name on the compliments jar. Glue on
special family photos and shapes cut from construction
paper or felt. Have each person write compliments
about every family member and put them in the jar.
Take turns reading compliments out loud. You may
even want to make this a regular event!

Encourage one another and build each other up.
1 THESSALONIANS 5:11 NIV

-Homemade Kazoos-

*Your family will make a joyful noise
with these homemade music makers!*

Materials:
Empty toilet paper or paper towel tubes
Markers for decorating
Waxed paper (cut into 6-inch squares)
Rubber bands

Allow each family member to decorate a paper tube
with markers. Cover one end of each paper tube with
waxed paper, securing the waxed paper with a rubber
band. Hum familiar songs into the open end. Take
turns conducting the kazoo choir.

-Feed the Birds-

*Experience nature right outside your window
by feeding birds with this simple craft project.*

Materials:
Pinecones   String
Creamy peanut butter   Birdseed

Tie a loop of string around the end of the pinecone.
Spread peanut butter all over the pinecone and dip it
in birdseed, coating completely. Hang pinecone bird
feeders in trees and watch as the birds come to feast.
Try to identify all the different bird species that show
up for a snack.

-Indoor Picnic-

*Can't go outside? Make the day fun for
everyone by having a picnic INSIDE!*

Necessities:
A cold or rainy day
A large blanket or tablecloth
Picnic basket filled with lunch
Board games

Spread out a large tablecloth or blanket on the living
room floor, preferably in front of a warm fireplace (if
you have one). Pretend you are going on a real picnic
and pack all the necessary supplies. Eat lunch as a
family and play your favorite games afterward.

*A cheerful heart brings a smile to your face;
a sad heart makes it hard to get through the day.*

PROVERBS 15:13 MSG

-Encouragement Boxes-

*This is a great way to get everyone in the
family involved in encouraging one another.*

Materials:
Shoe boxes
Tape
Glitter
Stickers
Pens, pencils

Wrapping paper or newsprint
Paints, markers, crayons
Glue
Stationery

Wrap each shoe box in newsprint or wrapping paper.
Wrap the lid separately so you can easily open the
box. Have each family member decorate a box. Make
them as elaborate as possible and make sure each box
is labeled with the person's name in big letters. Write
encouraging letters to each individual and put them
in the appropriate boxes. Keep your boxes and make
writing friendly notes a frequent activity.

*But encourage one another daily,
as long as it is called Today.*

HEBREWS 3:13 NIV

-"Name Above All Names" Poster-

Do you know all the names of God? Make a poster to remind everyone that He is Lord of all.

Materials:
Several Bibles
Large piece of poster board
Paint and markers

Work together to find names of God in the Old Testament. Allow each family member to take turns painting or writing a name on the poster. Add colorful designs and drawings to make your poster stand out. Hang the poster in a place where you will notice it often and remember to allow Jesus to be the Lord of your life.

God, the blessed and only Ruler,
the King of kings and Lord of lords.

1 TIMOTHY 6:15 NIV

-Homemade Cards-

*Your family can cheer someone
up with these homemade cards!*

Materials:
Construction paper   Markers
Glitter   Scissors
Glue   Stickers

Cut and fold the construction paper to your desired
size. Decorate with markers, glitter, and stickers. Add
encouraging scripture verses and take these cards to a
sick friend or neighbor. Or make a bunch of extra cards
and deliver them to a nursing home.

-A Puzzling Experience-

*Ready to tackle a challenge?
Create your own puzzles as a family.*

Materials:
Favorite posters or coloring pages
Glue
Heavy cardboard
Scissors

Glue coloring pages or posters to thick cardboard. After
they dry, cut them into puzzle pieces. Make each puzzle
increasingly more difficult. Each family member can
take a turn putting each puzzle together.

-Military Care Packages-

Prepare a care package for someone in
the military as a thank-you for serving.

Materials:
Shoe box
Hard candy
Pens and pencils
Instant coffee mix
Beef jerky
Toiletries, etc.

Fill a shoe box full of necessities and fun supplies
to thank someone in the service for protecting our
freedom.

Rescue me, O LORD, from evil men;
protect me from men of violence.

PSALM 140:1 NIV

-Make a Child Smile-

*Send pictures or letters to children
who are ill all across the country.*

Materials:
Crayons
Markers
Construction paper
Glue
Scissors

Get online and go to www.makeachildsmile.org. Here
you will find a list of children who are very sick, along
with their pictures, a description of their disease, and
a little personal information about them. Pick several
children and make a card or drawing for each one. Pray
for them as you make your cards, and let them know
that you will continue to do so.

> *Then little children were brought to Jesus for him
> to place his hands on them and pray for them.*
>
> MATTHEW 19:13 NIV

-Nature Walk-

Head outdoors with your family for some fresh air.
Experience the beauty of God's creation.

Necessities:
A nice fall day
Clear plastic bag
Bread for the ducks

Put on your walking shoes and plan a walk outside. As you are walking with your family, discuss the wonder of God's creation. Pick up special leaves, pebbles, and flowers as you go along and bring them home in your plastic bag for closer inspection. Don't forget to feed the ducks!

Many, O LORD my God, are the wonders you have done.

PSALM 40:5 NIV

-Bubbles and More Bubbles!-

Bubbles always bring out smiles!
Who can make the biggest bubble?

Materials:
1 cup dish soap
Water
Cookie cutters

Fill the kitchen sink with an inch or two of water and add a cupful of dish detergent. Mix well and use the cookie cutters to see who can blow the biggest bubble. Take pictures and award prizes for the best bubbles.

"But whoever drinks the water I give him will never thirst.
Indeed, the water I give him will become in him
a spring of water welling up to eternal life."

JOHN 4:14 NIV

-Crazy Pictures-

Make some great memories by taking crazy family photos.

Necessities:
Camera
Crazy outfits

Everyone should dress in color-coordinated outfits. Add glasses, fake mustaches, and other accessories so that you all look alike. Take funny pictures and then change outfits. Give each family member a turn with the camera. Set your camera's timer so you can have a few group shots, too.

A picture is worth a thousand words.

FRED BARNARD

-In the Garage with Dad-

Boys and girls are both interested in what Dad does in the garage. Fathers, it's time for a little show and tell.

Necessities:
Toolbox
Power tools
Lawn mower, generator, air pump, etc.

Take the family to the garage and let Dad show each tool and machine. If it is age-appropriate, allow each family member to try out the tool safely and with adult supervision.

> *Listen, my sons, to a father's instruction;*
> *pay attention and gain understanding.*
>
> PROVERBS 4:1 NIV

-Butterfly in the Sky-

Spend some time reading about and creating butterflies.

Materials:
Colored tissue paper
Pipe cleaners
Scissors

Cut tissue paper into small rectangles. Scrunch the center of the paper together and tie with a pipe cleaner. Twist and bend the pipe cleaner until you have what resembles a butterfly. Read *The Very Hungry Caterpillar* by Eric Carle together as a family.

> *Happiness is as a butterfly which, when pursued, is always beyond our grasp, but which if you will sit down quietly, may alight upon you.*
>
> NATHANIEL HAWTHORNE

-Chicken Day-

Today is a day to be goofy and celebrate chicken!

Necessities:
Music
Eggs
Chicken nuggets
A chicken dinner

Make everything today about chicken. Learn the chicken dance. Walk like a chicken and race each other around the house. Make eggs for breakfast, pack chicken nuggets for lunch, and have chicken for dinner. Watch the movie *Chicken Little* as a family after supper.

Do not count your chickens before they are hatched.

AESOP

-Go Fly a Kite-

Share this timeless activity with your children.
A fun time for a windy day!

Necessities:
A windy day
A kite
Open space to run

Take your family to the park to fly a kite on a clear day.
Make sure you are in a wide open space without power
lines or trees. Stand with your back to the wind and
hold up your kite. Let the line out a little. If there is
sufficient wind, your kite will go right up. Let the kite
fly away from you a little, then pull in on the line as the
kite points up so it will climb and find a good steady
wind.

> *Oh, that I had the wings of a dove!*
> *I would fly away and be at rest.*
>
> PSALM 55:6 NIV

-Pioneer Days-

Your kids will enjoy exploring the life of a pioneer.

Necessities:
A toy wagon   Beef jerky
Jug of water   Biscuits

Pretend you're a pioneer family. Pack food in a toy
wagon and take a walk. Stop for a meal and play
pioneer games like leapfrog or tic-tac-toe. Read
passages from historic novels.

-Pioneer Biscuits-

Continue the exploration with an authentic recipe.

Ingredients:
1 cup butter (no substitutions)
1 cup milk
4 eggs
3 cups flour
1 teaspoon salt
1 1/2 teaspoons baking soda
2 teaspoons cream of tartar

Mix all ingredients together. Make a thin loaf and
bake on a flat, greased pan. Bake at 350 degrees for 25
minutes. Serve warm with butter and honey. Look up
other pioneer recipes and eat like a pioneer all day!

-Your Own Holiday-

Your family is very special.
Celebrate this by inventing your own family holiday.

Necessities:
Camera
A unique day that belongs to no one else
Special events
Festive menu

Invent a unique holiday for your family. Decide what
to call the special day and celebrate it each year. Make
this day special. . .just for your family. Decide what
traditions you want to celebrate and plan a special menu
and fun activities. Take pictures to commemorate your
day. You might consider giving a family gift—
something that everyone can enjoy together: a new
camera, a board game, or a movie.

Let us make one point, that we meet each other with a smile,
when it is difficult to smile. Smile at each other,
make time for each other in your family.

MOTHER TERESA

-Be a Servant-

*Serving someone in need is an
incredible way to bond as a family.*

Necessities:
A servant's heart
Your local homeless shelter or church

Call your local homeless shelter or church to find out
how your family can help out. You will come away with
a renewed sense of love for each other and a thankful
heart.

-Give Away Day-

*Serve someone in need and instill
a sense of generosity in your children.*

Necessities:
Full closets
A cluttered toy room
Empty boxes

Have all family members go through their closets.
Choose at least five items from each to give away. Each
child should pick at least three toys to give away, too.
Donate the items and share your feelings about the
experience over lunch.

-Rhyme Time-

Make up your own rhymes.
You'll have a great time!

Necessities:
Pen
Paper
Dictionary
Thesaurus
Dessert

Recite as many nursery rhymes as you know, and
then make up your own. Read a Dr. Seuss book for
inspiration. Help each child look through the dictionary
or thesaurus to find words to rhyme. Have the family
members share their poems aloud and have a family
dessert reception afterward.

> *I know that there is nothing better for men*
> *than to be happy and do good while they live.*
>
> ECCLESIASTES 3:12 NIV

-Spaghetti Night-

Involve your whole family in preparing this basic dish.

Materials:
Favorite spaghetti recipe
Music
Red-checkered tablecloth
Table settings

Pretend you own an Italian restaurant. Involve the whole family in making the food and setting the table. Find some Italian music and take turns waiting the table. Find the words to "That's Amore" and sing it as you serve dinner. Tell your love story to your children while you eat.

I have told you this so that my joy may be in you and that your joy may be complete.

JOHN 15:11 NIV

-Band in a Box-

Make banjos out of boxes with this creative activity!

Materials:
Shoe box   Rubber bands
Costumes

Make a pretend banjo with a shoe box and rubber bands. Place the rubber bands over the lidless shoe box, spacing them a few inches apart. Try to make other instruments with household items. Form a band, change into costumes, and film your own music video.

-Road Trip-

*Put a little faith in your kids as you
allow them to plan this adventure.*

Materials:
State map   The Internet
Picnic lunch   Camera

Let your kids plan a one-day road trip. Get out the state map and look up various points of interest online. Consider state parks, rivers, museums, and nature trails. Let them pack a picnic lunch and take turns reading their directions to the driver from the backseat.

-Construction Zone-

*Construct stick houses and thank
the Provider for your own home.*

Materials:
Popsicle sticks
Wood glue

Your house is a home filled with love, laughter, and
thankfulness. Talk about these things as you create
popsicle stick houses with wood glue. Have each family
member "build" a room and then glue them all together
to make one large house. Don't forget the roof! Discuss
what it means to make a house a home.

*"Therefore everyone who hears these words of mine and puts them
into practice is like a wise man who built his house on the rock."*

MATTHEW 7:24 NIV

-Extra! Extra!-

*Family and loved ones far away will be
thrilled to read all about your family!*

Materials:
Paper
Pens or markers
Family photos
Glue

Write a newspaper freehand or take turns writing
articles on your computer or typewriter. Title the
newspaper using your last name. Include photos and
articles about recent family activities. Make sure there
are sections and pictures that include every family
member. Make copies to send to relatives and close
friends.

> *How beautiful on the mountains are the feet of
> those who bring good news, who proclaim peace,
> who bring good tidings, who proclaim salvation.*
>
> ISAIAH 52: 7 NIV

-A Day in Mexico-

*Spice up family night by turning your
house into a Mexican cabana for an evening.*

Materials:
Soft tortilla shells
Cheese
Tortilla chips
Salsa
Costumes

Have each family member research something about
Mexico. Assign one person to research food, another
dress, another customs, etc. Make quesadillas by
melting cheese inside the soft tortilla shells. Set out
chips and salsa and review what everyone learned.
Make a new Mexican dish and dress like an authentic
Mexican family. Don't forget the sombreros!

> *Glory in his holy name; let the hearts
> of those who seek the Lord rejoice.*
>
> PSALM 105:3 NIV

-Shoe Fun-

If the shoe fits. . .wear it!
If it doesn't, decorate it and show it off!

Materials:
Markers
New shoelaces
Glue

Shoes
Sequins
Puffy paint

Line up one shoe from each pair owned by your family and hide the others. The person who finds and matches the most shoes wins. Then decorate old sneakers with sequins and puffy paint and add new laces. Hold a fashion show to model the creations.

-Unbirthday Party-

Happy unbirthday to you!
Happy unbirthday to you!

Materials:
Birthday decorations
Birthday cake
Craft supplies

•

Hold an "unbirthday" party today. Decorate with leftover birthday decorations. Share homemade gifts made out of craft supplies. Bake a cake to eat and play party games.

-Luau Tonight-

Host a family luau and celebrate
Ohana—*family.*

Necessities:
Flower leis
Grass skirts
Pineapple
Barbecue food
Hawaiian music
Beach towels

Decorate your house or backyard Hawaiian-style. Have the entire family help prepare the food. Play musical beach towels using the same rules as musical chairs. The last beach bum on a towel is the winner!

*"The LORD your God is with you, he is mighty to save.
He will take great delight in you, he will quiet you with his love,
he will rejoice over you with singing."*

ZEPHANIAH 3:17 NIV

-Family Circus-

Turn your home into a circus—
even though it might already feel like one!

Necessities:
Costumes   Music
Peanuts   Cotton candy

Plan a family circus. Each family member may perform
one or more acts. If you have any pets, get them
involved by teaching them a new trick. Your circus
can be held indoors in a large open area or out in the
backyard on a nice day. Set a specific time for the circus
to begin and have bowls of peanuts and cotton candy
available for the audience.

-Family Parade-

A parade can always lift the spirits.

Necessities:
Bicycles   Toy wagons
Balloons   Streamers
Other decorations   Candy

Hold a bicycle-decorating contest and then ride in
a family parade. Decorate your bike or wagon with
streamers, balloons, and whatever else you can find.
Throw candy to each other as you ride down the street.
Let a neighbor or grandparent be the judge and award
prizes.

-The Berry Patch-

Berries are fun to pick. Put everyone to
work with this sweet family activity.

Necessities:
A berry patch
Good weather
Berry recipes

Go berry picking at a local berry patch. If that's not
possible, buy a variety of berries from the grocery store
and sample each kind. Decide which flavor is your
favorite. Have a contest. Find some berry recipes and
make pies or jam. Make extra and take some to your
neighbors.

Content makes poor men rich;
discontentment makes rich men poor.

BENJAMIN FRANKLIN

-Special Scrapbook-

*Create a special family scrapbook to archive
your memorable moments together and document
how everyone has changed and grown.*

Materials:
Blank scrapbook
Puffy paint
Decorations

Family photos
Glue or scrapbook tape
Scissors

Decorate the outside of the blank scrapbook with puffy
paint and decorations. Write your family's name on the
cover. Allow the cover to dry and then begin filling the
book with family memories. Each person can create
pages of your their own. Older family members can
help younger ones record dates and jot down details of
what's happening in each picture. Add new things to
the scrapbook every few months.

*"So commit yourselves wholeheartedly to these words of mine. . . .
Teach them to your children. Talk about them when you
are at home and when you are on the road, when you
are going to bed and when you are getting up."*

DEUTERONOMY 11:18–19 NLT

-Fishing Lessons-

Teach the timeless pastime of fishing to your children.

Materials:
Fishing pole   Sack lunch
Bait   Camera

Take your children to the nearest pond or river. Show them how to bait a hook and cast their line into the water. Pause for a lunch break. If you know how to clean and cook the fish, bring your catch home for dinner. If not, throw them back in—but take a picture first!

-The Aquarium-

*Discover the amazing colors and
diversity that God created in fish!*

Necessities:
Local aquarium   Crayons or markers
Paper   Seafood dinner

Visit your local aquarium. Most big cities have one, but if an aquarium isn't accessible to you, go to the library and rent a nature documentary on fish. Draw your favorite sea animals, and plan a seafood dinner with your children.

-The Joke's on You-

Have some fun making up silly jokes during dinner.

Necessities:
Dinner
Pen
Paper

Before dinner, have each family member write down
a question that begins with the word *why* on a slip of
paper. Then, on a separate slip of paper, have each write
down a completely different answer beginning with the
word *because*. Do not answer the question that you've
just asked. Then put all the "why" questions in a hat and
all the "because" answers in another. Mix them up and
pull out one of each. Read them both aloud at dinner.
You'll get some pretty random, crazy jokes!

> *The human race has one really effective weapon,*
> *and that is laughter.*
>
> MARK TWAIN

-Read a Book, Deliver a Smile-

*Record your favorite book on tape and
send it to someone who could use a smile.*

Materials:
Favorite book
Tape recorder
Blank tape

Take turns reading one of your favorite books aloud.
Record it on tape and deliver it to a shut-in or a friend
or relative who is ill. Make sure all family members gets
to say something on the tape, even if they can't read.

*May God, who gives this patience and encouragement,
help you live in complete harmony with each other,
as is fitting for followers of Christ Jesus.*

ROMANS 15:5 NLT

-Green Day!-

"Go green" with your family in an unusual sort of way.

Materials:
Crayons   Markers
Green foods   Green face paint

Get a box with sixty-four crayons and pick out all the different shades of green. Draw a picture that uses as many shades of green as possible. Do the same with markers. Paint your face green, wear green clothes, and eat all green foods for supper!

-I Spy Championship-

Remember this old game? Make it a little more challenging.

Materials:
Paper   Pencils

This championship can take place indoors, outdoors, or both. For the first round, play it the old-fashioned way: One person picks something in the room, and everyone else has to guess what it is. For the second round, pick one person to "spy" five things, and everyone must write down their guesses. For round three, go outside and have everyone write down action verbs that they can see: someone jogging, a squirrel eating, etc. The family member that writes down the most verbs is the winner. Award prizes.

-Friendly Snowball Fight-

Who doesn't love to play in the snow?
Head outdoors for this challenge.

Necessities:
Sunny day
Snowballs or cotton balls
Glue

Head outside on a sunny day for a friendly snowball fight. If you don't have snow in your area or if it's the middle of summer, make your own "snowballs" by gluing a bunch of cotton balls together. Split into teams and have fun tossing "snow" at each other. Take a break for hot chocolate in the winter or iced tea in the summer.

One kind word can warm three winter months.

JAPANESE PROVERB

-Pajama Time-

No matter how old your children are,
everyone appreciates being cuddled now and then.

Necessities:
A large bed
Your pajamas
Favorite book

Spend a lazy day in bed with your whole family. Keep your pajamas on and cuddle up to each other in the biggest bed in the house. Take turns reading your favorite books to each other. Have pizza delivered or warm up leftovers so nobody has to do any work. Relax and rest as a family!

"Come to me, all you who are weary and burdened,
and I will give you rest."

MATTHEW 11:28 NIV

-Breakfast for Supper-

Switch things up a bit and serve breakfast for supper!

Materials:
Pancake mix
Blueberries or chocolate chips
Bacon or sausage
Eggs

Gather the whole family in the kitchen and teach them how to scramble eggs, fry meat, and flip pancakes. Make the pancakes into funny shapes and make faces on them with blueberries or chocolate chips. Serve the meal for supper!

-Supper for Breakfast-

Switch things up even more and serve supper for breakfast!

Materials:
Individual pizza crusts
Pizza toppings

Make a special breakfast pizza. Let each family member have a small crust to cover with whatever toppings that person likes. Can't stomach pepperoni for breakfast? Try a Hawaiian pizza with pineapple and ham.

-Crazy Beans-

*Add creativity and beauty to your
walls with these "bean mosaics."*

Materials:
Dried multicolor beans
Glue
Construction paper
Frames

Arrange the dried multicolor beans close together in
various designs on the construction paper. Glue them
to the paper and allow to dry. Put the mosaics in frames
and hang them all over your house. Make up a poem
about beans. Eat beans and wienies for supper.

*There is neither Jew nor Greek, slave nor free,
male nor female, for you are all one in Christ Jesus.*

GALATIANS 3:28 NIV

-Learning Braille-

Teach your family something new by learning braille.

Materials:
Paper
Hole punch
Copy of the braille alphabet (found online)

Find an online copy of the braille alphabet. Write secret messages to your family members using a hole punch for the dots. Each person deciphers the secret message's code. When it's time for dinner, Mom or Dad should write a message that reads, *Clean Up!*

-Confetti Collection-

Punch holes in colored paper to make confetti for parties, games, and celebrations.

Materials:
Colored paper
Hole punch
Confetti cake mix

Gather all of the holes you punched out while making your braille messages and start a collection. Make more confetti by punching holes out of colored paper. Use your confetti at birthday parties, sporting events, or during a family parade. Eat confetti cake while tackling this project.

-Tea Party-

*Bring out your fancy china and
a spot of tea with your family.*

Materials:
Tea
China cups
Finger sandwiches

Brew a pot of tea and have everyone in the family help
make finger sandwiches: peanut butter and jelly, tuna,
chicken salad, and egg salad. Remove the crusts and cut
into bite-size pieces. Set the table with your best china
cups and remind children to be very careful with them.
Put on some elegant music, dress up a little, and meet
your family at the kitchen table for tea.

*If this is coffee, please bring me some tea;
but if this is tea, please bring me some coffee.*

ABRAHAM LINCOLN

-A Day to Dream-

*Spend today sharing and discussing
your dreams and hopes for the future.*

Materials:
Poster board
Magazines
Scissors
Glue

Cut out pictures for a collage of dreams you have for
the future. Discuss everyone's goals and the steps each
will need to take to accomplish those goals. Encourage
everyone to nurture these dreams.

*"For I know the plans I have for you," declares the LORD,
"plans to prosper you and not to harm you,
plans to give you hope and a future."*

JEREMIAH 29:11 NIV

-Backward Day-

You will feel a little backward after today!

Necessities:
Books
Mirror

Enjoy a backward day. Get out of bed backward, put your clothes on backward, and walk backward around the house. Eat dessert first. See how many family members can read a book backward by holding it up to a mirror. Find out what other things you can accomplish backward.

-Create a Hat-

Encourage your children's creativity by letting them design their own hats.

Materials:
Plain baseball cap from a craft store
Puffy paint

Let family members use the puffy paint to decorate their hats however they like. Put as many hats as possible on your head and read *The 500 Hats of Bartholomew Cubbins* by Dr. Seuss for inspiration.

-What Do You Smell?-

*Play this smelly game and find out
whose nose can sniff the most smells.*

Materials:
Blindfold
A variety of objects that have a scent

Play a smelly game. Gather a variety of fragrances such
as orange, vanilla, hot chocolate, perfume, soap, etc.
Blindfold family members separately and let them guess
the fragrances. The family member who guesses the
most scents correctly wins a stinky prize!

*Smell is a potent wizard that transports you across
thousands of miles and all the years you have lived.*

HELEN KELLER

-Edible People-

*Prepare to get sticky as you make
a giant marshmallow man to eat!*

Materials:
Toothpicks
Marshmallows
Mini marshmallows
Icing tubes
Licorice

Make people figures out of toothpicks, marshmallows, and licorice. Make faces with decorative icing, and have a contest to see who can make the biggest marshmallow man. Take pictures of your creations and enjoy.

*Recommend to your children virtue;
that alone can make them happy, not gold.*

LUDWIG VAN BEETHOVEN

-Obstacle Course-

Rise above obstacles in your own backyard course.

Materials:
Orange traffic cones
Ropes
Chairs
Hula-hoops

Create a backyard obstacle course using traffic cones, ropes, chairs, and Hula-hoops. Have contests to see who can go through it the fastest. Change the course after the first contest and try it again. If you have pets, try to lead them through it as well.

-Pamper Your Pets-

Spend extra time with your family pet today.
It'll make your pet's day. . .and your family's, too!

Necessities:
Your family pet(s)   Special animal treats
Pet toys

Spoil your pet today! Buy your pets a new toy or a special treat and make up new games to play with them. If your family doesn't have any pets, visit a pet store or make up an imaginary pet. Give it a name and draw a picture of it to hang on your refrigerator.

-What's in a Name?-

The Bible tells us our names are important. . .
find out what each name in your family means.

Necessities:
A Bible
Internet access
Pens, pencils
Paper

Every name has a meaning. Research each name in your family, including your last name, and find out its origins and what it means. Is your name from the Bible? Find out! Tell your children why you decided to give them the names that they have. Make up your own family "coat of arms" and create a special symbol to identify your family. Consider having it printed professionally on a flag or a T-shirt.

A good name is more desirable than great riches.

PROVERBS 22:1 NIV

-Learn Spanish-

Your family members will enjoy changing their names for a day and learning something new in Spanish.

Materials:
Spanish dictionary
Internet access

Look up simple words in a Spanish dictionary or online. Teach your family to say "please" and "thank you," and give everyone a Spanish name. Everyone in the family gets ten *centavos* (pennies). Someone who calls someone else by his or her regular name loses a centavo. Whoever has the most centavos at the end of the day wins.

-Foil Creations-

See how creative you can be with foil.

Materials:
Aluminum foil
Timer
Camera

Give every family member a roll of foil. Set a timer for five minutes and see what everyone can make. Have each person explain what their creation is and take lots of pictures. For dinner, make a foil pocket and add chicken, vegetables, and spices for a yummy meal.

-Cloud Pictures-

*Use your imagination to
discover pictures in the clouds.*

Necessities:
A fluffy cloudy day
Several large blankets

Spread some blankets out on the grass in your backyard
or at the park and lie down to gaze up at the sky. Name
the clouds. See how many pictures you can see in the
clouds. Have every family member tell a story using the
clouds to illustrate. Talk about any airplane trips you've
taken through the clouds. Describe what they look like
from above.

*Look up at the heavens and see;
gaze at the clouds so high above you.*

JOB 35:5 NIV

-Saved for a Rainy Day-

Rainy days don't have to be glum!
Make your next rainy day the best.

Necessities:
A rainy day
Raincoats and boots
Popsicle sticks
Glue
Crayons
Paper

Start the day by going outside to splash in the puddles.
Sing in the rain. After getting thoroughly wet, come
inside to warm up and change clothes. Read the story of
Noah's ark from the Bible. Color a rainbow. Build your
own ark out of popsicle sticks and glue.

> *"Whenever the rainbow appears in the clouds, I will see it*
> *and remember the everlasting covenant between God*
> *and all living creatures of every kind on the earth."*
>
> GENESIS 9:16 NIV

-Picnic at the Playground-

Most parents take their kids to the park and sit close by to watch. This time, do everything with them!

Necessities:
A nice day
Sack lunch

Take your family to the park and do everything together. Race down the slides together. Who can swing the highest? Can the kids push parents on the merry-go-round? Break for a lunch in the grass and then get back to playing!

-Make Your Park Beautiful-

Be a servant today and clean up trash at your local park.

Materials:
Large trash bags
Gloves

Head to your local park to do some cleanup work with your family. Pick up all the trash that you see, but be sure to wear gloves. Teach your family the importance of preserving God's beautiful creation.

-Truth or Dare-

*Get to know your family even
better with this interesting game.*

Necessities:
An honest family
Special snacks

Settle on the couch with some special snacks and get in
the mood to learn more about your family. Play "Truth
or Dare." One family member asks a question; the
others either tell the truth or complete a "dare." Make
sure there's parental supervision to avoid any risky dares.

*For your love is ever before me,
and I walk continually in your truth.*

PSALM 26: 3 NIV

-Biblical Brothers and Sisters-

*Get your children interested in
some great stories from the Bible.*

Materials:
The family Bible

Look up stories of famous brothers and sisters in the
Bible (e.g., Miriam, Aaron, and Moses or Martha,
Mary, and Lazarus). Take turns reading about these
famous siblings. Share a story about brothers and sisters
in your family. Conclude the evening by praying for
each other to be the kind of family that God wants you
to be.

-Paper Plane Race-

Paper airplanes are always fun to make. Let 'em fly!

Materials:
Paper
Crayons, markers

Teach your children how to make paper airplanes.
Practice flying them and see whose plane goes the
farthest. Make more planes and color them with
crayons and markers. See if new designs make any
difference in the way they fly.

-Respect the Elderly-

*Teach your children the importance of showing
respect to the elderly in your community.*

Necessities:
Local senior center or nursing home
Colored pictures
Small gifts

Visit a nursing home as a family. Call ahead and find
out how many residents live there. Take inexpensive
gifts: some fruit, a potted plant, or a homemade item.
Younger children can color pictures to give away. Stop
and talk to the senior residents and you might just make
a few new friends. You might even join them in playing
a game or two.

> *"Rise in the presence of the aged, show respect for
> the elderly and revere your God. I am the Lord."*
>
> LEVITICUS 19:32 NIV

-Laughing Limericks-

Make each other laugh with silly made-up limericks.

Materials:
Pens or pencils
Paper

Compose a limerick about each member of your family.
A limerick is a five-line humorous poem that uses
rhythm and rhyme. Make a list of words that rhyme to
help out younger family members. Read your limericks
aloud and plan to be thoroughly amused. Set them to
music and make silly songs out of them.

Each one should use whatever gift he has received to serve others,
faithfully administering God's grace in its various forms.

1 PETER 4:10 NIV

-House Calls-

*Pretend to be a doctor with your
family and make a house call.*

Materials:
Band-Aids   Toy stethoscope
Thermometer   Lollipops

Pretend to take a trip to the doctor's office: check blood
pressure, take temperatures, and give shots and Band-
Aids. Let each family member take a turn playing
doctor. Everyone gets a lollipop after a pretend shot!

-Stargazing-

*Generations of people have been mesmerized by the stars.
Share this experience with your family.*

Materials:
A clear night   Warm blankets
Black construction paper   Silver star stickers
Silver glitter   Glue

Pick a clear night and lie on warm blankets to gaze
up at the stars. See how many constellations you can
identify. After everyone is back inside, use black paper,
stars, and glitter to make pictures of the night sky.

-Banana Split Night-

Go bananas over this fun activity.

Materials:
Vanilla and chocolate ice cream
Bananas
Chocolate syrup
Whipped cream
Maraschino cherries
Serving platter

Find a large serving platter and let each family member make a section of a giant banana split. Sit around the table with spoons and dig in. Think of all of the words that rhyme with banana and make up a poem. See how many splits each person in the family can do when you are finished eating.

But the fruit of the Spirit is love, joy, peace, patience, kindness, goodness, faithfulness, gentleness and self-control.

GALATIANS 5:22–23 NIV

-Bonjour, Français!-

Expand your knowledge with another language:
Say, "Hello, French!"

Materials:

French dictionary

Drawing paper

French recipes

Pens, pencils

Use simple French words such as bonjour, *oui* and *merci* today. Eat French food like crepes, quiche, and crème brûlée. Go online and find out interesting things about French culture. Make a drawing of the Eiffel Tower.

-Family Car Wash-

There's nothing like getting the
whole family wet during a car wash!

Materials:

Buckets

Water

Water hose

Sponges

Soap

Give everyone a sponge and pull the cars out onto the driveway. Let the little ones work at the bottom of the cars and the older kids and adults work on the top. Make sure everyone gets thoroughly drenched. See if the neighbors would like to have their cars washed, too.

-Role Reversal-

*Give your kids a chance today to find out
what parenting is like. . .switch roles!*

Necessities:
Open-minded parents
Responsible children

Children will pretend to be the parents today. Let
them make breakfast, lunch, supper, and all the plans
throughout the day. The children can tell you what to
do, and you'll have to obey or suffer the consequences.
At the end of the day, call a family meeting to find out
what your children learned about responsibility and
what the parents remembered about being a kid.

Children are a gift from the LORD; they are a reward from him.

PSALM 127:3 NLT

-Watermelon Bash-

Enjoy some good times with this fun summer fruit.

Materials:
Two large watermelons
Knife
Watermelon bubble gum

Purchase two large watermelons. Cut the melon into slices. Save the seeds and have a seed spitting contest outside. Chew watermelon bubble gum. See who can blow the biggest bubble. Instead of "hot potato," try to play the game with a watermelon.

-Radio Show-

*Making up your own radio show is so much fun,
you won't want the day to end!*

Materials:
Tape recorder   Paper
Pen, pencils   Music

Broadcast a family radio show. Listen to your favorite radio stations for inspiration, and give everyone a role. Write news articles about your community and your family's recent adventures. Tell a joke or have someone pray and read devotions. Record your show on tape and save it as a keepsake.

-Just Because-

Make this day all about your family. . .just because!

Necessities:
Paper
Pens, pencils
The family piggy bank
Calendar

Have a "just because" day. Each family member should write a suggestion on a piece of paper of something to do as a family today. Think of ideas to help you stay within the budget. You might have enough money to go see a movie together, but instead of going out for ice cream afterward, stop by the grocery store and buy items to make your own sundaes at home. After everyone has written down a suggestion, take a vote. Save the other ideas and plan "Just Because" days throughout the year with the remaining ideas.

Be kind and compassionate to one another.
EPHESIANS 4:32 NIV

-Indoor Campout-

Bring the excitement inside with an indoor campout.

Materials:
Tent
Sleeping bags
Pillows
Flashlights
Marshmallows
Chocolate candy bar
Graham crackers

Put up a small tent in the living room. Pretend you are in the middle of the forest having a campout. Make s'mores in the microwave, turn off all the lights, and tell stories with the flashlights on. End the evening by praying for each other and gathering inside the tent for a cozy night's sleep.

> *And the LORD God made all kinds of*
> *trees grow out of the ground.*
>
> GENESIS 2:9 NIV

-Homemade Play Dough-

*Make your own play dough and use it
to create anything you can imagine.*

Materials:
1 cup flour   ¼ cup water
¼ cup salt   Food coloring

Mix flour and salt in a bowl and then add water and
food coloring. Knead and squeeze the dough into a
claylike consistency. You may need to add more water.
Make different shapes with your dough. Seal in a plastic
bag when you are finished playing with it.

-Buried Treasure-

Create an adventure right in your own home.

Materials:
Paper   Small treats and prizes
Crayons or markers   Pirate costumes

Hide treats around the house, mark them on a treasure
map, and take turns seeking the treasure. Remember: *X*
marks the spot! Dress up and talk like pirates while you
search for the treasure.

-Emergency Day-

Does your family know what to do in an emergency?
Make a game out of this important information!

Materials:
Emergency phone numbers
First aid kit
Fire escape plan

Imagine that you are hiking in the woods. What will
you do if you get lost? Do you know what to do in case
of an emergency? What if someone gets hurt? Make
up several emergency scenarios and have your children
respond. Make sure everyone knows what to do by
showing the fire escape plan for your home, handing
out lists of emergency phone numbers, and pointing out
your designated family meeting place.

In the same way your Father in heaven is not willing
that any of these little ones should be lost.

MATTHEW 18:14 NIV

-Sponge Art-

Is your family into fashion?
Design your own T-shirts with sponges.

Materials:
Water
Sponges
Scissors
Fabric paint
Plain white T-shirts
Cardboard

Dip the sponges in a small amount of water to make them moist and pliable. Cut sponges into several different sizes and shapes. When you're ready to paint, slip a piece of cardboard inside the T-shirt so the paint doesn't seep through the material. Then dip the sponges in paint and start making designs on your T-shirt. Wait for your designs to dry and have everyone wear their T-shirts out to dinner.

Create in me a pure heart, O God,
and renew a steadfast spirit within me.

PSALM 51:10 NIV

-You've Been Slimed-

Ready to get messy?
Make some silly slime with your family.

Materials:
Drop cloth
Cornstarch
Water
Food coloring

Place a drop cloth around the area you plan to get messy. Mix 1 cup of cornstarch with 1 cup of water and a few drops of food coloring. Mix it with your hands until you get a smooth texture. You can change the texture by adding a second cup of cornstarch or by boiling the water. Parents will definitely need to supervise the slime slinging. Once you are finished playing and experimenting, store the slime in an airtight container for up to three days.

"I am the one who made the earth and created people to live on it.
With my hands I stretched out the heavens.
All the stars are at my command."

ISAIAH 45:12 NLT

-Kitchen Music-

Discover musical instruments in your own kitchen!

Materials:
Water glasses
Water
Pencil

Fill glasses with different levels of water. Line them up together on the counter. Tap the filled glasses with a pencil to make different notes. Make up a song. Take turns arranging your own music. Play duets. Try to play "Happy Birthday" and "Jesus Loves Me."

> *Let us come before him with thanksgiving*
> *and extol him with music and song.*
>
> PSALM 95:2 NIV

-Follow the Compass-

This activity can be an exciting adventure for everyone!

Materials: Pen
Paper   Compass

Give your children directions using only compass points, such as "walk two blocks north." Write the directions down and follow your kids as they figure out which way to go using the compass. After a few tries, steer your kids toward someplace fun like a park.

-Food Groups-

Let your children plan and prepare a well-balanced meal using all four food groups.

Materials:
Information about the food pyramid (found online)
Recipes
Food from the grocery store
Paper
Pencil or pen

Let your children plan a balanced meal. Have them find recipes, write down their menu, and create a shopping list. Take them to the grocery store and let them select the ingredients. Help them prepare the meal when you return.

-Alphabet Soup-

Make today all about the alphabet.
Where did it come from? Why do we need it?

Materials:
Internet access
Paper
Pen, pencils
Alphabet soup

Research where our alphabet came from online or at
the library. Who invented it and how? Design your
own alphabet, choosing a picture symbol for each letter.
Write your names and special messages with your own
alphabet. Eat alphabet soup for lunch.

You yourselves are our letter, written on our hearts,
known and read by everybody.

2 CORINTHIANS 3:2 NIV

-Do You Hear What I Hear?-

*Play this game while teaching your children
the truth about rumors and gossip.*

Necessities:
The Bible
Your family

Direct your family to sit in a circle. Whisper a sentence
in your child's ear. Have the child repeat it to the next
person in the circle. Repeat until everyone has heard
the sentence, and ask the last person to say aloud what
they heard. How has the sentence changed? Point out
how repeating "rumors" can cause confusion and spread
false information. Look up verses in the Bible that talk
about rumors and gossip. Discuss how gossip can hurt
someone else's feelings.

*A gossip betrays a confidence,
but a trustworthy man keeps a secret.*

PROVERBS 11:13 NIV

-Time Capsule-

*Bury a time capsule in the backyard
to create memories for the future!*

Materials:
Sturdy metal box   Paper
Items from around the house

Choose items for a time capsule. Gather special trinkets
and photographs, and have family members write a
letter to themselves in the future. Write down the date
and time that you created this time capsule. Bury the
container in your yard and make a note to dig it up
again in ten, twenty, or even thirty years from now.

-Family Tree-

Share important lessons from the past.

Materials:
Paper   Pens or markers
Family photos

Draw a family tree. Add photos of family members.
Tell stories from your childhood. Talk about some of
the important lessons that God has taught you along
the way. Share some lessons that your own parents or
grandparents have shared with you.

-A Corny Day-

*Set aside a day to celebrate and
enjoy this traditional staple food.*

Materials:
Corn-based recipes
Paper
Pen or pencil

Look up corn-based recipes and head to the grocery
store for ingredients. Plan to make a variety of foods
that incorporate corn in its many forms: corn tortillas,
corn on the cob, popcorn, etc. Tell "corny" jokes during
dinner. Walk through a cornfield or tackle a corn maze
after dinner if one is nearby.

*Farming looks mighty easy when your plow is a pencil,
and you're a thousand miles from the corn field.*

DWIGHT D. EISENHOWER

-Collect Stamps-

Stamps have seen the world!
Create a poster and trace their origins.

Materials:
Mail

Save your incoming mail for a few weeks. Cut the
stamps off the envelopes and glue them to a poster.
Study the envelopes to find out where the stamps have
been. Look at a map and imagine all the places the
stamps could have gone before arriving at your house.

-Handprints-

Give your kids a "hand" with this keepsake project.

Materials:
Construction paper   Permanent marker
Finger paint   Picture frame

Make handprints on construction paper with finger
paint. Include a hand from every family member. Label
and date underneath each hand using a permanent
marker. Frame the handprints and hang them on the
wall for all to see!

-Cotton Ball Art-

Need another creative way to paint?
Use cotton balls!

Materials:
Cotton balls
Nontoxic paint
Small bowls
Construction paper
Glue

Divide different colors of paint into small bowls. Dip cotton balls into the paint and create pictures on the construction paper. Try dipping the cotton balls in more than one color. See what happens. Set the cotton balls in a safe place to dry and then glue them to some more construction paper to create a picture.

Every artist dips his brush in his own soul,
and paints his own nature into his pictures.

HENRY WARD BEECHER

-DIY-

*Every member of the family likes to be helpful
and will enjoy the simple things each can
do to help fix things around the house.*

Materials:
Paper
Pen or pencil
Toolbox
Duct tape

Lightbulbs
Glue
Scissors

Fix it yourself today. Make a list of all the things that
need repaired around the house. Have your children
assist in simple jobs like patching a wall, changing a
light bulb, or putting gas in the car. Make sure you talk
to your family about safety while you are repairing or
fixing anything.

*All hard work brings a profit,
but mere talk leads only to poverty.*

PROVERBS 14:23 NIV

-The Apple of Your Eye-

*Learn about apples and eat apple pie. . .
with the apples of your eye.*

Materials:
Apples
Apple recipes

Take your family to an orchard and go apple picking. If
there isn't an orchard close to you, go to a grocery store
or a farmer's market instead. Examine all the varieties
of apples. Buy your favorite and involve the children in
preparing the apples for an apple pie or another favorite
apple dish.

*Keep me as the apple of your eye;
hide me in the shadow of your wings.*

PSALM 17:8 NIV

Evergreens

Evergreens can symbolize eternal life.
Use this time to share the message of
Christ with your family.

Necessities:
A nice day
An evergreen forest
Your car
Evergreen guidebook or Internet information
Paper
Crayons or markers

Walk or drive through a forest and identify different evergreens. See if you can find the tallest one. Learn how tall evergreens can grow and how long they can live. Talk about the "evergreen" eternal life that Jesus came to give. Draw pictures of the evergreens you saw when you get back home.

"For God so loved the world that he gave his one and only Son,
that whoever believes in him shall not perish but have eternal life."

JOHN 3:16 NIV

-Puppet Family-

Your own show—starring you!

Materials:
Brown paper bags
Yarn
Glue
Video recorder
Scissors
Fabric
Markers

Make puppets out of paper bags. Decorate them with yarn and fabric to make them look like your family. Write a play with all of the members of your family, but switch roles so everybody is using someone else's puppet. Film the show and watch it together.

-Match the Mittens-

Make your own wintertime matching game!

Materials:
Construction paper
Crayons or markers
Scissors
Hot chocolate
Stopwatch

Draw pairs of mittens on construction paper. Decorate each pair exactly the same and cut them out. Mix them together and look for matching pairs. Make hot chocolate with marshmallows and have a championship tournament. The person who finds all the matches fastest, wins!

-Mission to Mars-

Everyone dreams of going to outer space.
Pretend to take your family to Mars!

Materials:
Play dough
Construction paper
Markers or crayons
Large work area
Space food

Pretend that you are taking a trip to Mars. What do you
need to take? What might you see? Make a topographic
map of Mars, using play dough to form mountain
ranges. Remind your kids that God created Mars and
everything in the universe. Eat space food. Space ice
cream is always a good choice!

Let the heavens rejoice, let the earth be glad;
let the sea resound, and all that is in it.

PSALM 96:11 NIV

-Hello? Hello?-

Make this old-fashioned toy with soup cans and string.

Materials:
Empty soup cans
String
Screwdriver
Hammer

Parents should punch a hole in the bottom of each empty soup can using a screwdriver and a hammer. Link the cans together by attaching one end of a very long piece of string to the hole at the bottom of each can. Have two people stand far apart, each holding one of the cans. Have one person speak into the can and the other person hold the other up to an ear. Can you hear if someone is talking on the other end?

> *Good leaders cultivate honest speech;*
> *they love advisors who tell them the truth.*
>
> PROVERBS 16:13 MSG

-Twenty Questions-

Develop your investigative skills.

Materials:
Paper
Pen, pencil

Have everyone write down a word or a phrase on a piece of paper. No peeking! Family members should take turns guessing what word or phrase you have written by asking yes or no questions. Whoever guesses the word or phrase correctly gets to go next.

-From the Dog-

Spend a day in the life of your pet.

Materials:
Family pet
Paper
Pen

Follow your pet around for a few hours and find out what it does all day. Write a story about your family from your pet's point of view. Talk about all of the members of the family and what your pet likes or dislikes about each one.

-Random Acts of Kindness-

Wake up this morning intent on doing secret and special things for everyone in the family.

Necessities:
The ability to keep a secret
A weekend day

Inform your family the night before that the next day will be "random acts of kindness" day at your house. Everyone should seek to do secret and thoughtful things for each other. Someone should definitely volunteer to make dinner for Mom and mow the lawn for Dad. While you are eating supper, discuss your day and how each one felt receiving kindness and giving it back to each other.

> *"Then your Father, who sees what is done in secret, will reward you."*
>
> MATTHEW 6:6 NIV

-Happy Bird Day!-

Celebrate our flying feathered friends today!

Materials:

Binoculars	Paper
Pens or pencils	Crayons or markers
Beads	Fabric
Feathers	Glue

Do a little bird watching with your family this morning. Head outside your house or to the park with your binoculars and spy on our flying feathered friends. Draw and decorate a picture of your favorite bird. Look online and find out more about the birds in your area.

-Purple for Peace-

Plan a peaceful day. . .discussing peace and doing activities that symbolize peace.

Materials:

Purple foods	Purple crayons,
Bible	markers, or paint
Construction paper	Purple clothes

Wear purple for peace today. Eat purple food like grapes and eggplant. Discuss what "peace" really means. Look up verses in the Bible that talk about peace and make a purple poster illustrating what you've read. Pray for countries at war.

-What's in the Bag?-

Good surprises are always wonderful!
Surprise your family with food and fun.

Materials:
Familiar objects from around the house
Paper grocery bag full of items to make a favorite meal

Put several familiar items in a bag. Have family members reach inside and try to identify the objects by touch. Fill up a paper grocery bag with ingredients to make one of your family's favorite meals. Pull out one item at a time and allow them to guess what the meal might be. Begin preparing the meal as the family keeps guessing. Whoever guesses correctly gets to help make dinner. Those who guess incorrectly have to do all the dishes after dinner!

They devoted themselves to the apostles' teaching and to the
fellowship, to the breaking of bread and to prayer.

ACTS 2:42 NIV

-Red Light, Green Light-

This game is always known to bring out a smile.
Add homemade stop and go signs to make
things more interesting.

Materials:
Red and green construction paper
Crayons, markers, or paint

Play "Red Light, Green Light." Make stop and go signs
and choose one family member to be the traffic officer.
Everyone should line up on one side of the room or
yard while the traffic officer stands at the other end.
When the officer says, "Green light!" and holds up
the go sign, everyone walks quickly toward the traffic
officer. When the traffic officer says, "Red light!" and
holds up the stop sign, everyone freezes. Whoever
doesn't stop is out. Keep up the game until someone
reaches the traffic officer or only one person is left. That
person becomes the traffic officer and the game starts
over.

Would you like to live without fear of the authorities?
Do what is right, and they will honor you.

ROMANS 13:3 NLT

-Scrabble It!-

Help your family discover all the amazing
Scrabble-based activities you can do together.

Materials:
Several games of Scrabble
Wood glue
Flat wooden picture frames
Family photos or original artwork

Purchase several old games of Scrabble at a thrift store.
Start off by playing a traditional game of Scrabble.
Then divide the alphabet tiles among all of your family
members. What words can you create with the letters?
Find some family photos or create some original works
of art and put them in flat wooden frames. Use the
Scrabble letters to personalize the frames with your
name or with a title for your artwork. Glue the tiles to
the wooden frame. Keep one for yourself and give some
away as gifts.

It's a job that's never started that takes the longest to finish.

J.R.R. TOLKIEN

-Healthy Heart-

Discover ways to keep your family in good health.

Materials:
Internet access
Printer
Paper
Pens or pencils
Fresh fruits and vegetables

Locate a picture of the cardiovascular system online and print it out. Talk with your children about what makes a healthy heart. Discuss ways that your family can stay healthy. Have your family write out a healthy grocery list. Eat fresh fruits and veggies for a snack.

Dear friend, listen well to my words; tune your ears to my voice. Keep my message in plain view at all times. Concentrate! Learn it by heart! Those who discover these words live, really live; body and soul, they're bursting with health.

PROVERBS 4:20 MSG

-Designer Stationery-

Send a smile in the mail today!

Materials:
Paper

Envelopes

Crayons

Markers

Stickers

Ribbon

Design your own stationery by adding stickers and hand drawn pictures to blank sheets of paper. Bundle the sheets with envelopes and tie with a ribbon. Write a letter to your grandparents and send them this homemade gift in the mail.

-Fun with Feet-

Whose feet are the fastest?

Necessities:
Clean feet

Ruler

Paper

Stopwatch

Pencils

Trace your feet on a sheet of paper. Measure to see whose are biggest and whose are smallest. Have a timed race in the backyard to see whose feet are fastest. See how many everyday things you can do with your feet. . . like painting, peeling a banana, etc.

-Field Day-

Host a family field day.
Don't forget the prizes!

Necessities:
A nice day   Yardstick
Stopwatch   Balls
Jump ropes   Prizes

Have a family field day. Who can jump the highest?
Run the fastest? Throw the farthest? Who can jump
rope the longest without tripping or getting tired?
Award prizes and celebrate each and every family
member's achievement. Write down the stats to
compare with next year's results.

Do you not know that in a race all the runners run, but only one
gets the prize? Run in such a way as to get the prize.

1 Corinthians 9:24 NIV

-Pie Time-

Pie for a game and pie for a snack!
Take pleasure in pies today.

Materials:
Paper plates
Markers
Brads
Pie

Play a pie game: Use a marker to divide a paper plate
into six numbered sections so that it resembles a pie.
Use a brad to attach a spinner. Take turns spinning and
see who gets the highest score. Eat a slice of fresh pie
for a snack.

What calls back the past, like the rich pumpkin pie?
JOHN GREENLEAF WHITTIER

-Cookies in the House!-

Nothing makes your house smell better than fresh-baked cookies! It puts everyone in a good mood, too!

Materials:
Favorite cookie recipe
The necessary ingredients
Paper
Crayons

Get everyone into the kitchen to help bake a favorite cookie recipe. Explain where the recipe came from and have everyone share why it's the favorite. Plan a delicious meal to accompany your dessert.

-Charades-

You can really get your creative juices flowing with this "gesture only" game!

Necessities:
A nice open space for acting out the words

Divide into teams and play charades. Choose simple words, people, or events from the Bible and act them out without speaking. A point is earned every time a team guesses what's being acted out. Whoever has the most correct guesses, wins.

-The Extra Mile-

Go above and beyond today!
Show your family what it means to "go the extra mile."

Necessities:
The Bible (preferably a study Bible)
Paper
Pens or pencils

Read Matthew 5 together as a family. If you have a study Bible, read the footnote commentaries about this chapter. Discuss what Jesus was teaching us through this chapter. Have family members write down their own thoughts. Then discuss ways that you can go the extra mile for your family and for other people in your life. Each person should write down ways to go above and beyond for specific people and set target dates as goals to have done something special for that person. A month from now, come back together as a family and discuss the outcome.

If someone forces you to go one mile,
go with him two miles.

MATTHEW 5:41 NIV

-Love Is the Greatest-

Celebrate the love that your family has for one another!

Materials:
Pink and red construction paper
Crayons or markers
Pencils or pens
Scissors
Cake mix
Heart-shaped
   baking pan
Icing

Cut out construction paper hearts and write notes to your family members, telling what you love about each one. Bake a heart-shaped cake and decorate it. Discuss Jesus' love for us over dinner.

-Fairy Tales-

Start a tradition and share your favorite childhood fairy tales with your children.

Materials:
A book of fairy tales
Costumes

Read or tell one of your favorite fairy tales to your children. Put on costumes and act out the stories.

-What Time Is It Mr. Wolf?-

*You'll work up quite an appetite after playing
this exciting game with your family!*

Necessities:
A large play area

In this game, one player is the wolf. The wolf stands
with their back turned to the others at the opposite end
of the yard or room. The others call out, "What time is
it, Mr. Wolf?" and the wolf turns to face everyone and
shouts out a time. If the wolf says it's "10 o'clock," then
the others would take 10 steps toward the wolf. If the
wolf says it's "2 o'clock," then they would take 2 steps,
and so on. The wolf will continue to turn their back to
the group until someone gets close enough to the wolf.
Then the wolf will turn around and shout "DINNER
TIME!" and run after everyone. Anyone who makes it
back to the starting line is safe, but whoever the wolf
catches is the next wolf.

When the boy is growing he has a wolf in his belly.

GERMAN PROVERB

-Musical Old Maid-

Rediscover an old game with a new twist.

Materials:
"Old Maid" cards
CD player and music CDs

Play a musical version of "Old Maid". Take turns being the one to decide when the music stops. Distribute all the cards among everyone. When the music stops, the last person to stand up takes a card from everyone else. The first person without cards wins.

> *You are worried about seeing him spend his early years in doing nothing. What! Is it nothing to be happy? Nothing to skip, play, and run around all day long? Never in his life will he be so busy again.*
>
> Jean-Jacques Rousseau

-What's the Weather?-

*Pretend you are a family of meteorologists
and make up your own weather report.*

Materials:
Internet access or your local TV news
Paper
Markers or crayons

Give your own weather report today. Look up your local
weather online or watch your local news on TV to find
out the seven-day forecast. Draw a big map and add
appropriate symbols, such as rain, snow, or sunshine.
Take turns giving the report.

The best thing one can do when it's raining is to let it rain.

HENRY WADSWORTH LONGFELLOW

-Don't Forget Your Manners-

*Have fun pretending to be a pig today,
but don't forget your manners!*

Materials:
Paper
Pens or pencils
Ham sandwiches
Pork dinner
Pig-themed movie

Pretend to be a pig today. Say "oink, oink" instead of "yes." Eat ham sandwiches for lunch. Draw a picture of a pig in a barnyard. Eat pork for your evening meal. After dinner, watch a movie starring a pig like Babe or Miss Piggy.

After dinner sit awhile after; supper walk a mile.

English Proverb

-Fancy Frames-

*Display your family's artwork in
one-of-a-kind picture frames.*

Materials:
Old or inexpensive picture frames   Fabric
Fabric glue   Buttons
Ribbon   Glitter
Other craft decorations   Dessert
Original artwork   Music

Wrap the picture frames in fabric, and decorate with
buttons, ribbon, glitter, etc. Display original artwork in
the frames and set up a family art show. Serve dessert
and play music while everyone is looking at the art.

-Honor Your Teachers and Coaches-

*Let your child's teachers and coaches
know how much you all appreciate them.*

Materials:
Construction paper   Envelopes
Stickers   Glitter
Glue

Use construction paper to make a card for each of your
children's teachers and coaches. Parents should write a
note on the inside at the top and kids can write a note
at the bottom.

-Smorgasbord Night-

*Get rid of leftovers and have fun
as a family at the same time!*

Necessities:
Leftovers
Board games

Pull out all of the leftovers in the refrigerator. This is
especially nice to do after a holiday when you have a
lot of leftover food. Let each family member make up
a personal culinary creation. Take turns tasting each
other's recipes. Write down the good ones to try again
another time. Play board games afterward.

> *I know that there is nothing better for men
> than to be happy and do good while they live.*
>
> ECCLESIASTES 3:12 NIV

-Leapfrog-

Hop around with your loved ones and get a little silly!

Materials:
Green construction paper
Scissors

Make your own lily pads by cutting them out of green construction paper. Jump like frogs. Practice jumping on all fours from one "lily pad" to another. Play "leapfrog" by jumping over other family members. If you're really adventurous, try eating frog legs for supper!

*The miracle is not to fly in the air,
or to walk on the water, but to walk on the earth.*

CHINESE PROVERB

-Habitats-

Research the habitats of your local animal friends.

Necessities:
A local park
Notepad
Pens or pencils
Camera
Internet access or your local library

Take a walk in the park. Look for plants and animals that live there. Write them down on a notepad. Take pictures and do some research online. What do these plants or animals need to grow? Does anything threaten their survival?

Animals are such agreeable friends—
they ask no questions, they pass no criticisms.

GEORGE ELIOT

-Money Hunt-

*You can always find some loose change in the laundry
or in the couch. Use this money for something special.*

Materials:
An empty jar

Search for pennies and other loose change all day. Look
on the floor as you go to the grocery store. Look in
the parking lot. Check your couch and look in all your
pants pockets. Set aside all the money you find for a
special church offering.

> *Be generous: Invest in acts of charity.*
> *Charity yields high returns.*
>
> ECCLESIASTES 11:1 MSG

-A House of Cards-

Get out all of the card games in the house for this activity.

Materials:
Several different card games
Snacks

Find all of the card games you have in the house or go to the thrift store and buy a few. Spend the day learning new card games and playing old ones. Divide into teams and play a tournament.

-A Day with the Grands-

*Call up the grandparents and plan
for a trip down memory lane.*

Necessities:
Tape recorder or video camera
Blank tape

Visit grandparents and learn how they celebrated certain holidays when they were children. Find out what games they played and ask them to teach you how to play. Record their responses on a blank video or cassette tape to save as a keepsake. Take a special gift to thank them for being wonderful grandparents.

-Learn Morse Code-

Learn a new language!

Necessities:
Internet access
Dark evening
Flashlight

Look up Morse code online or at your library. Learn how to send a message using the code. Take turns sending secret messages in Morse code using a flashlight. Find out the history of Morse code and discuss how this might be helpful in an emergency.

> *For the LORD gives wisdom, and from*
> *his mouth come knowledge and understanding.*
>
> PROVERBS 2:6 NIV

-Your Personal Bill of Rights-

*Develop a personalized Bill of Rights for
your family and allow everyone to take part.*

Materials:
Notepad
Pens or pencils
A copy of the Bill of Rights

Introduce your children to the Bill of Rights. Look up
its history and discuss its significance. Compose a bill
of rights for your family. Let everyone's voice be heard,
and then take a vote on what should be included in your
family Bill of Rights.

*Anyone, then, who knows the good
he ought to do and doesn't do it, sins.*

JAMES 4:17 NIV

-A Day to Try Something New-

Try something you've never done before.

Necessities:
Your local library

Take the entire family to the library. Family members should pick out a "do-it-yourself" book about something they have never done before. For example, one child could pick out a recipe book and try to make something new in the kitchen. Dad could check out a book about a home remodeling project that he's never tried before, etc.

-Laundry Day-

Show everyone that laundry can be fun!

Materials:
Dirty laundry
Laundry soap
Washer/dryer

Make a game out of sorting the dirty laundry. Take turns putting loads in the washer and dryer and helping each other fold the clothes. Sing songs and reward your family for helping with a necessary household chore.

-Bean Raffle-

*Raffle off some household items
to your own family members!*

Materials:
Dried beans
A few new items bought at a discount store

Hold a bean raffle. Have Family members go to their
rooms and find five things they would like to raffle off.
Add a few inexpensive new items from a discount or
thrift store. Give each person an equal number of dry
beans. Let them bid beans for their favorite items. The
highest bidder wins each item.

> *Kindness is the language which the
> deaf can hear and the blind can see.*
>
> MARK TWAIN

-Celebrate Chocolate!-

Get ready for a taste-testing adventure!

Materials:
A variety of chocolates
Pens or pencils

Paper
Movie

Purchase several different varieties of chocolate: milk chocolate, dark chocolate, fruit-flavored chocolate, truffles, etc. Taste them all and decide which one is your favorite. Rate them on a scale of 1 through 5, with 1 being the best and 5 being the worst. Compare answers with your family. Watch a movie about chocolate, like *Charlie and the Chocolate Factory*.

-Stick Friends and Family-

Good friends and family stick together!

Materials:
Popsicle sticks
Construction paper
Poster board

Markers
Yarn
Glue

Make a "stick family." Family members should decorate a craft stick with markers, yarn, or construction paper so that it resembles themselves. Glue the sticks to poster board and display it. Then family members should make a few sticks that resemble their friends and add those to the board, too.

-We Love Eggs-

Do something interesting with eggs today.
Try a new dish or play a fun game that incorporates them.

Materials:
Eggs
Spoons

Make eggs for breakfast. After breakfast, hard-boil some eggs. Save some for eating and some for play. Give each family member a hard-boiled egg and a spoon and head outside. Designate a starting line and a finish line. Race each other with a spoon in your mouth and an egg on your spoon. Whoever reaches the finish line with the egg still on their spoon, wins. If your egg falls on the way to the finish line, you have to start back at the beginning. Eat egg salad or deviled eggs for lunch.

To eat an egg, you must break the shell.

JAMAICAN PROVERB

-Poem Illustrations-

*Put poems into pictures with
this meaningful activity.*

Materials:
The Bible
A book of poems from the library
Construction or drawing paper
Crayons, markers, or paint

Read several long poems as a family. Consider reading
Psalm 119 or *The Song of Hiawatha*. Think about
what the poems mean to you and then illustrate them.
Compare your illustrations when you are finished and
discuss what your illustration means to you.

*Blessed are they who keep his statutes
and seek him with all their heart.*

PSALM 119:2 NIV

-Mine Your Yard-

Pretend you are a miner and explore your own backyard. What treasures can you find?

Materials:
Wagon or wheelbarrow
Small garden shovels
Sculpture glue from a craft store

"Mine" your yard. Collect rocks and sticks in your wagon or wheelbarrow. Parents should mark off a small area of the yard where it is okay to dig. Show the kids how to use a shovel and look for yard treasures. Make a sculpture out of whatever you find.

Attitude is a little thing that makes a big difference.

WINSTON CHURCHILL

-Fun with a Camera-

*Have a blast with a disposable camera
and create some lasting memories.*

Materials:
Disposable camera
Construction paper
Stapler
Tape or glue

Buy a disposable camera. Go for a walk or drive and take turns using the camera. Develop the film and make a book about your trip. Staple several sheets of construction paper together to make your scrapbook. Tape or glue your pictures in the book. Take turns journaling about the pictures.

Fill your paper with the breathings of your heart.

WILLIAM WORDSWORTH

-Yummy Fun in the Snow-

Get a little silly to keep from getting chilly!

Necessities:
A nice snowy day
Warm coats and gloves

Flavored fruit drinks
Cups or mugs

Bundle up and head outside to gather cupfuls of clean white snow. Cover the snow with flavorings to make your own snow cones! Divide up each person's snow cone so that everyone can have a taste of the various flavors. If you don't have snow in your area, crush some ice or use a shaved ice machine to make your own snow cones indoors!

-Homemade Balderdash-

Make up your own dictionary game.

Materials:
Dictionary
Pens or pencils

Paper

Choose words from the dictionary and have everyone make up crazy definitions. Everyone should write the pretend definitions on slips of paper and someone else should write down the correct definition from the dictionary. Put all the definitions in a hat and then read them aloud. Vote on which definition you think is correct.

-Funny Photos-

*You'll have plenty of goofy pictures
after this zany activity!*

Necessities:
Dress-up clothes
Gaudy accessories
Camera
Homemade invitations

Make invitations to invite your close friends and family
to your house for a "one-of-a-kind" family portrait. Ask
them to wear their most outrageous outfits. Raid your
drawers and closets to find the most hideous looking
accessories to use as props. Take funny pictures of
everyone who shows up. Have the pictures developed
or printed and let everyone know when they will be
available for pickup.

*Imagination was given to man to compensate him for what
he is not; a sense of humor to console him for what he is.*

FRANCIS BACON

-Tongue Twisters-

Crack up with your family as
you try these tongue twisters.

Materials:
A book of tongue twisters
Notepad
Pens or pencils

Find a book of tongue twisters at the library or look
them up online. Go around the room and have your
family members say as many as they can as fast as they
can. Try to write your own tongue twisters by making
each word begin with the same letter.

He who guards his mouth and his
tongue keeps himself from calamity.

PROVERBS 21:23 NIV

Button Up

*See how many interesting things
you can do with buttons!*

Materials:
Buttons
Needle
Thread
Scissors
A clear jar

Look for shirts with lots of buttons. Which one has
the most? Teach your children how to sew on a button
using a needle and thread. Fill a jar with buttons and
have a contest where family members guess how many
buttons they think are in the jar. When the votes are in,
count them and the person who guessed closest to the
actual number, wins!

*Remember, O LORD, your great mercy and love,
for they are from of old.*

PSALM 25:6 NIV

-All about Poland-

What do you know about Poland?
Experience Polish customs with your family.

Materials:
World map
Internet access
Polish music
Paper
Pens or pencils
Polish sausage

Find the nation of Poland on a world map. Research Poland online and find out about its culture. Listen to music by Polish composers, such as Chopin or Paderewski. Draw a picture while you're listening. Eat Polish sausage for dinner.

Even a clock that does not work is right twice a day.

POLISH PROVERB

-Family Cookbook-

Share your yummy recipes.

Materials:
Favorite family recipes
Paper
Markers or crayons

Make a cookbook featuring your family's favorite recipes. Ask grandparents and relatives for recipes from their own kitchens. Who has the oldest recipe? Which recipe do you like the best? Illustrate the recipe book with drawings and colored pictures of the finished meals and make copies to use as gifts.

-Stuffed Animal Roundup-

*Gather your stuffed animals and pets
to re-create a story from Genesis.*

Materials:
Bible
Stuffed animals
Pets

Read Genesis 2:1–20 as a family. Use your family pets and all the stuffed animals you have in the house to tell the story of Creation. Like Adam, name the animals.

-Hair Salon-

*Girls love to have their hair done, but even Dad
will enjoy a new style at your family's hair salon.*

Materials:
Hair spray
Combs, brushes
Hair gel
Temporary hair dyes
Towel
Hair accessories

Clean up the bathroom and place a kitchen chair in
front of the bathroom mirror. Put a towel around the
shoulders of each "customer." Fix everyone's hair in a
different style. Experiment with temporary hair dyes,
hair gels, and hair spray.

*"The LORD does not look at the things man looks at. Man looks at
the outward appearance, but the LORD looks at the heart."*

1 SAMUEL 16:7 NIV

-Go Nuts!-

*Celebrate the peanut today with
all the "nuts" in your life!*

Materials:
Peanut butter
Peanuts
Chocolate
Internet access
Paper
Pens or pencils

Eat peanut butter sandwiches for lunch. Get online and learn about the one hundred uses George Washington Carver found for the peanut. Cover peanuts with chocolate. Write silly jokes about peanuts.

*The greatest oak was once a little
nut who held its ground.*

UNKNOWN

-Family Powwow-

Travel back in time to explore Native American culture.

Materials:
Popsicle sticks
Glue
Fabric
Native American recipes

Research Native Americans online or at the library. Play a game about Native Americans by matching housing, clothing, and geographical regions with particular tribes. Pick your favorite tribes and dress up like them. Build yourself a Native American home using popsicle sticks or fabric. Look up recipes and create an authentic Native American meal.

The LORD loves righteousness and justice;
the earth is full of his unfailing love.

PSALM 33:5 NIV

-Mileage and Expenses-

Learn while having a great time on a family day trip.

Materials:
Notepad
Pens or pencils
Envelope
Calculator

Take a day trip out of town: visit a relative, go to a park or a museum, etc. Show your children how to track mileage and expenses. Keep all your receipts from the day in an envelope. When you get home, calculate how much the trip cost. Come up with a budget for your next family activity.

> *If you want children to keep their feet on the ground, put some responsibility on their shoulders.*
>
> ABIGAIL VAN BUREN

-Goodies for a Good Cause-

*Make someone else's day by delivering
goodies to people who could use a lift!*

Materials:
Church directory
Greeting cards
Homemade goodies

Spend the day baking homemade goods to give to
others. Call the secretary at your church and ask for
a list of names of people who are ill or are in need of
cheering up. Write notes of encouragement and deliver
homemade goodies in person. Take the time to pray for
and with each person you visit today.

-Tomato Time-

*Find a way to make tomatoes interesting
and appealing to each family member.*

Materials:
Fresh tomatoes   Tomato sauce
Tomato juice   Tomato recipes

Eat fresh tomatoes and use tomato sauce in your
family's dinner. Drink tomato juice with lunch. Find
recipes containing tomatoes, and let each family
member make a special tomato dish.

-Plants Galore-

Beautify your home with plants and flowers.

Materials:
Indoor and outdoor plants
Potting soil
Pots
Gardening gloves
Hand shovels and trowels

Take the family to your local garden center or home improvement store. Purchase a variety of indoor and outdoor plants. Plant flowers all around the house, inside and out. Let family members pick a special plant to adopt and take to their room. Remember to feed and water your plants regularly to keep them healthy.

*Take thy plastic spade, it is thy pencil;
take thy seeds, thy plants, they are thy colours.*

WILLIAM MASON

-Learn to Juggle-

*Juggling is a fun activity that
improves hand-eye coordination.*

Materials:
Tennis balls
Scarves
Other items to juggle

Start juggling with two balls. Once you get the hang of
that, add another ball. See who can juggle the longest
without dropping any balls. Try juggling scarves. Which
is easier? Hold a contest. The winner gets to choose
what meal to have for dinner.

*Show us your unfailing love, O LORD,
and grant us your salvation.*

PSALM 85:7 NIV

-Walk Away the Day-

*Enjoy being together as a family
as you get some good exercise.*

Necessities:
A nice day
Good walking shoes
Water bottle

As much as possible, walk everywhere you go today.
Make sure you stretch first and have on a good pair of
walking shoes. Take along a water bottle as well. If you
live out in the country and walking into town isn't an
option, take a long walk with your family.

*Me thinks that the moment my legs begin to move,
my thoughts begin to flow.*

HENRY DAVID THOREAU

-Pictures Tell a Story-

Use your imagination to write a story using magazine and newspaper clippings.

Materials:
Magazines
Newspapers
Paper
Pens or pencils

Look through old magazines and tear out pictures that look interesting. Write a one-page story about each picture you choose. Display the pictures and the stories together. Read each story aloud. Now look through magazines or newspapers and find articles that don't have any pictures. Draw pictures to go with those articles.

The Possible's slow fuse is lit By the Imagination.

EMILY DICKINSON

-Conservation at Home-

Conserving energy is an important and cost-effective practice that can be a lot of fun!

Materials:
Paper plates
Chips
Candles

Cold cuts
Fresh veggies

Find ways to conserve energy at home. When it gets dark, try lighting up your home with candles. Turn off the TV off and play a game instead. Use recyclable paper plates and eat low-waste foods like cold cuts, fresh veggies, and chips.

-Pool Party-

Whether it's summer or winter, take your family to the pool to play in the water.

Necessities:
A local pool
Swimming attire
Pool games

Take your family to a local indoor or outdoor pool and go swimming. Play Marco Polo and other fun pool games. Challenge each other to swimming races and cannonball contests. Who can make the biggest splash?

-Celebrate Cats-

*There are many different kinds of cats in the world.
Expand your knowledge of these furry felines.*

Necessities:
Kittens
A library

Celebrate cats. Visit a neighbor or a pet store that has
kittens. Go to the library and look for pictures and
books about cats. Is a lion part of the cat family? What
about a tiger or a bobcat? Find out everything you can
about cats. Get a nature movie about the feline family
from the library.

*If animals could speak, the dog would be a blundering
outspoken fellow; but the cat would have the rare
grace of never saying a word too much.*

MARK TWAIN

-A Meal of Rice-

*In many third world countries, people don't even
have rice to eat. Pray for these people as you
give up a meal to help the hungry.*

Materials:
Rice

Eat rice for one meal today. Give the money that you
saved to an organization that helps the hungry. While
you are eating the rice dinner talk about how each
person wuld feel if they didn't have food or a home to
live in. Pray for opportunities to help others in need.

> *"For I was hungry and you gave me something to eat,
> I was thirsty and you gave me something to drink,
> I was a stranger and you invited me in."*
>
> MATTHEW 25:35 NIV

-Summer Plans-

*This activity should be done on a weekend
right before school lets out for the summer.*

Materials:
Family calendar
Pens or pencils
Notebook

Celebrate summer. Stay up until the sun goes down
and make plans for the summer season. Get out the
family calendar and plan at least two or three extra
special activities for each month of summer. Start a
list of things you will need for these activities in your
notebook. Plan a budget and have everyone commit to
saving their spare change to help pay for these events.

A life without love is like a year without summer.

SWEDISH PROVERB

-Hollerin' Contest-

Cheer your family on in your own special way.

Necessities:
The great outdoors

Hold a hollerin' contest. Who can yell the loudest?
Who has the most unusual holler? Make up a family
cheer. Make up a cheer for each individual family
member using that person's name. Make sure you do
this activity at a time when it will not disturb your
neighbors. Or take your family to a place where it won't
matter how loud you are.

> *We will shout for joy when you are victorious and
> will lift up our banners in the name of our God.*
>
> PSALM 20:5 NIV

-American Folktales-

*Discover America's roots and
some early song and dance steps.*

Materials:
A book of American folktales   Fabric
Poster board   Glue
Folk music   Biscuits
Coffee

Read or tell your family an American folktale like *Paul
Bunyan* or *Johnny Appleseed*. Glue fabric cutouts to
poster board to make a picture that illustrates the story.
Learn several American folk dances. Make homemade
biscuits and allow your children to have a little taste of
coffee.

-Love Those Cows!-

*Many of our everyday foods come from cows.
Celebrate cows today!*

Materials:
Cowbell   Milk
Cheese

Hold a "mooing" contest. Eat a grilled cheese sandwich
and drink a cup of milk for lunch. Pick at least two
more dairy products to have with your dinner. What
kind of dessert could you make from cow's milk? Take
turns ringing a cowbell to announce dinner.

-Fun with Hula-Hoops-

Hold a Hula-hoop contest and
invent some new games.

Materials:
Hula-hoops
Stopwatch
Music

Twirl Hula-hoops and play jumping games with them.
Hold a contest to see who can Hula-hoop the longest.
Keep some upbeat music playing in the background. Take
turns making up new games!

> *Satisfy us in the morning with your unfailing love,*
> *that we may sing for joy and be glad all our days.*
>
> PSALM 90:14 NIV

-Ice Cream in a Bag-

There's nothing like a family activity
that is also quite yummy!

Materials:
Ice cubes
1 gallon-sized plastic food storage bag
6 tablespoons rock salt
½ cup whole milk
¼ teaspoon vanilla
1 tablespoon sugar
1 pint-size plastic food storage bag

Fill the gallon-size bag half full of ice and add rock salt. Put milk, vanilla, and sugar into the small bag and seal it tightly. Place the small bag inside the large one, and seal it tightly. Shake until the mixture is ice cream, about 5 minutes. Wipe off the top of the small bag with a washcloth and open it carefully. Enjoy!

I scream, you scream, we all scream for ice cream!

AMERICAN PROVERB

-Busy Bees-

Enjoy the by-products of the busy bees in your world.

Materials:
Yellow and black construction paper
Scissors
Biscuits
Honey

Buzz like bees: Use the *Z* sound instead of an *S* in your words. Create your own bee out of yellow and black construction paper. Serve honey with biscuits. Discuss what to do if you ever get stung by a bee and how to prevent bee stings.

> *How doth the little busy bee*
> *Improve each shining hour,*
> *And gather honey all the day*
> *From every opening flower!*
>
> ISAAC WATTS

-Man on the Moon-

*Let your imagination run wild as you
enjoy one of God's magnificent creations!*

Materials:
Calendar
Blanket
Thermos of hot chocolate
Mugs

Check your calendar to find out when there will be a
full moon. Take a blanket to sit on and a thermos of hot
chocolate to go moon gazing in your backyard. Make
up stories about traveling to the moon and the man in
the moon.

*When I consider your heavens, the work of your fingers, the moon
and the stars, which you have set in place, what is man that you
are mindful of him, the son of man that you care for him?*

PSALM 8:3–4 NIV

-Thread the Needle-

Play a game and have an important family discussion.

Necessities:
A large open playing area or backyard
Bible

Play a game called "Thread the Needle." Family
members form two lines and hold hands while one
person crawls underneath the hands. Continue until
everyone has had a chance to thread the needle. Discuss
what Jesus meant when he talked about the camel going
through the eye of a needle.

-All-Stars-

*Everyone in your family is a star—
let them shine with personalized badges!*

Materials:
Construction paper
Markers
Two-sided tape

Celebrate your family's all-stars. Make badges using
construction paper and two-sided tape. Have them
all read "#1 in _____" (fill in the blank to personalize
the badges). Go out for a special meal and wear your
badges.

-Dog Days-

*Act like a family of dogs today
and make a doggie collage.*

Necessities:
Poster board
Magazines
Glue

Work like a dog today. Carry things in your mouth, wiggle, and pant. If you have a dog, enjoy an outing with your pet. If not, go for a walk and look for dogs. Vote on what everyone's favorite breed is. Cut out pictures of dogs from a magazine and make a collage.

Jesus replied: "Love the Lord your God with all your heart and with all your soul and with all your mind."

MATTHEW 22:37 NIV

-Twins! Twins!-

*Look out for twin pairs today and
make your own matching game.*

Materials:
Construction paper
Markers
Scissors

Watch for twins today: anything (people, houses,
clothing, etc.) that has an identical pair. Make your own
matching game. Draw pictures of twins with markers on
construction paper. Cut them out and turn them over on
a table. Whoever can find the most matches, wins.

*There are two things in life for which
we are never truly prepared: twins.*

JOSH BILLINGS

-Potato Stamps-

Make your own stamps out of potatoes!

Materials:
Fresh potatoes
Poster paint
Poster board
Blunt pencil
Sharp knife
Paintbrush

Cut a large potato in half and dry it off. With a pencil, poke a shape or design into the potato and cut away the excess with a knife. Dry off the potato again. Apply paint to the potato stamp and press onto the poster board. Make as many different stamps as you can.

"The Father loves the Son and has
placed everything in his hands."

JOHN 3:35 NIV

-Mouth Montage-

*Learn about a new art form today and
create a montage with your family.*

Materials:
Old magazines
Glue
Scissors
Internet access

Cut out pictures of people's smiles and make them into
a montage. Creating a montage involves combining
pictures from various sources to give the illusion that
the elements belonged together originally. Look up
examples of montages online before you begin.

*May the words of my mouth and the meditation of my heart be
pleasing in your sight, O LORD, my Rock and my Redeemer.*

PSALM 19:14 NIV

-Friendship Bracelets-

*These friendship bracelets will look
fabulous and are fun to make, too!*

Materials:
Embroidery floss or yarn
Transparent tape

Make family friendship bracelets. Pick four different
colors of yarn or floss. Cut the strands evenly and knot
them at the top. Tape the top to a table so it will stay
in place as you work. Weave the strands together into
unique designs.

-Exploding Soda-

*Your kids will wonder why you are letting them
get so messy in this interesting experiment.*

Materials:
Bottles of soda
Garbage bags
Dictionary
Ice cream

Go outside, shake up a soda bottle, open it, and watch it
spew. Wear plastic garbage bags over your clothes. Look
up carbonation in the dictionary. What does it mean?
Drink soda floats afterward and enjoy!

-A Day at the Airport-

Spend a day at the airport with your family. . .
without going on a trip!

Necessities:
Local airport

Go to a local airport and watch airplanes arrive and depart. Make up a story: "I'm going on a trip to ____ and I'm taking _____." Make the words begin with the same letter. If the airport has a restaurant, eat there for lunch and discuss an upcoming family vacation.

> *The air up there in the clouds is very pure and fine,*
> *bracing and delicious. And why shouldn't it be?*
> *It is the same the angels breathe.*
>
> MARK TWAIN

-Respect the Elderly-

Seek out wisdom from the elderly people in your life.
Honor and respect them.

Necessities:
The library

Celebrate senior citizens. Research famous seniors at
the library. Talk about what you want to be like when
you are old. Visit the oldest member of your family.

> *"Is not wisdom found among the aged?*
> *Does not long life bring understanding?"*
>
> JOB 12:12 NIV

-Ride the Wind-

Wind can be very powerful. . .and fun, too!

Necessities:
A slightly windy day
Balloons filled with helium
Picnic lunch

Ride the wind today. Release a helium balloon and
watch it sail into the sky. Eat a picnic lunch in the park.
When you get back home, look for pictures of things
carried by wind (kites, hot air balloons, gliders, etc.)
Why is wind necessary?

> *He let loose the east wind from the heavens
> and led forth the south wind by his power.*
>
> PSALM 78:26 NIV

-Garage Sale Contest-

You can always find a great bargain at a garage sale.
Turn bargain-hunting into a contest!

Necessities:
Five dollars for every family member
Local garage sales

Everyone in your family should start with five dollars each. Go to at least two or three different garage sales and see how many items you can get for five dollars. The person with the most items wins. Make a rule that you can only buy something you would actually use, so each person must give a reason for their purchases.

"No one can serve two masters. For you will hate one and love the other; you will be devoted to one and despise the other. You cannot serve both God and money."

MATTHEW 6:24 NLT

-Mouse Games-

*A loose mouse in the house can cause a fright,
but mouse games can be a lot of fun!*

Materials:
Paper
Pen or pencil

Cheese or cheese crackers
Mouse-themed movie

Play a mouse word game. Think of a word related to
mice and draw a line for each letter, just like you would
play hangman. For each correct guess, eat a tiny piece
of cheese or a cheese cracker. Watch a movie starring
Mickey Mouse or another famous mouse.

-Golden Days-

*Yellow means sunshine and smiles.
What a wonderful color!*

Materials:
Yellow clothes
The game "Clue"
Yellow crayons and markers

Yellow foods
Paper

Wear yellow. Cook a meal that includes yellow
ingredients. Take turns playing the part of Colonel
Mustard in the game of Clue. Make a yellow picture
with crayons and markers.

-Musical Scales-

Aren't you glad God created music?

Materials:
Paper
Pens or pencils
Piano or other instrument

Teach your children the names of the spaces on the treble clef (F, A, C, E). Make as many words as possible out of the letters A through G, the seven letters used for the musical scale. Play them on a piano or another instrument. Learn an easy song like "Hot Cross Buns" or "Three Blind Mice."

Sing and make music in your heart to the Lord.

EPHESIANS 5:19 NIV

-The Height of Fun!-

Discover the height of fun and the fun of height!

Materials:
Wooden blocks
Drawing paper
Pens or pencils
Tape measure

Climb to the top of the tallest public building in your town. At home, see how high you can build a skyscraper out of blocks. Draw a skyscraper. Measure how tall everyone is in your family.

> *You've got to do your own growing,*
> *no matter how tall your grandfather was.*

IRISH PROVERB

-Uncle Sam-

*Learn about Uncle Sam and celebrate
our American mascot.*

Materials:
Paper
Pens or pencils
Crayons or markers
Internet access

Celebrate Uncle Sam today. Look for images of the
American symbol and research the history of Uncle
Sam. What was his purpose? Draw and color your own
picture of him or tell a story about him. Eat something
red, white, and blue today.

*I like to see a man proud of the place in which he lives.
I like to see a man live so that his place will be proud of him.*

ABRAHAM LINCOLN

-Rock Collection-

Start a family rock collection.

Materials:
Wagon
Book about rocks
Box
Paints or other decorations

Pick up a book about rocks at the library. Go for a walk with a wagon and pick up different rocks. Sort them into igneous, sedimentary, and metamorphic. Decorate a sturdy box to keep your rock collection. The next time you take a special trip with your family, gather more rocks as souvenirs for your collection.

> *On Christ, the solid Rock, I stand;*
> *All other ground is sinking sand,*
> *All other ground is sinking sand.*
>
> EDWARD MOTE

-Candy Fun-

Candy can become a work of art!

Materials:
Solid plastic cups | Glue
Small pieces of candy | Poster board

Hide candy under one of three cups. Move the cups around. Guess which cup hides the candy. The person who guesses correctly gets to eat the candy. Glue pieces of candy together to make a sculpture. Use the wrappers to make a collage on a piece of poster board.

-Celebrate Autumn-

Fall is a wonderful season full of color.

Materials:
Paper | Apple cider
Crayons or markers | Calendar

Celebrate autumn. Write down five favorite things about fall. Use fall colors to illustrate the list. Rake leaves and jump in them. Drink apple cider and plan a day to visit a pumpkin patch and a local football game.

-Open Mic-

Every family has at least one comedian.
Humor each other today!

Materials:
Comic book
Joke book
Paper
Colored pencils
Toy microphone
Snacks

Read a comic book together. Write a comic strip about your family using colored pencils. Gather your kitchen chairs into the living room and set out snacks. Choose family members to go up to the mic and do a comedy routine. Read or make up your own jokes.

Humor is the great thing, the saving thing.
The minute it crops up, all our irritation and resentments
slip away, and a sunny spirit takes their place.

MARK TWAIN

-Rabbits and Bunnies-

Hop to it!

Materials:
Paper
Crayons or markers
Glue
Cotton balls
Carrots
Carrot recipes

Hop like a rabbit. Draw a picture of a rabbit and add cotton balls for soft ears and a cotton tail. Eat carrot sticks as a snack. Look up carrot recipes and make something yummy for supper or dessert. Why are carrots good for your eyes? Do you think carrots make rabbits see better and hop faster?

If you chase two rabbits, you will not catch either one.

RUSSIAN PROVERB

-Macaroni Mosaic-

Macaroni makes a great meal. . .
and a great piece of art!

Materials:
A variety of pasta, including macaroni
Cheese sauce
Glue
Poster board
Yarn
Scissors

Assemble a variety of pasta shapes and glue them to poster board to make pictures. Be sure to use different colors of pasta, too. Make jewelry out of pasta. Cut pieces of yarn and string pieces of pasta together. Serve macaroni and cheese for dinner.

The more you eat, the less flavor;
the less you eat, the more flavor.

CHINESE PROVERB

-Groove to the Beat-

*Add a little rhythm to you day
by making your own drums.*

Materials:
Empty cans
Cardboard containers or pots and pans
Wooden spoons
Upbeat music

Make drums out of empty cans and cardboard
containers or pots and pans. Use your hands to beat the
drums. Now try wooden spoons. Which makes a better
sound? Drum along with your favorite music.

*Praise him with the clash of cymbals,
praise him with resounding cymbals.*

PSALM 150:5 NIV

-TV Producer-

Write, direct, and star in your own TV show!

Materials:
Paper   Pens or pencils
Video camera   Blank tape
Popcorn

Produce an original episode of your favorite television show. Assign characters to your family. Write down parts for each person to say. Record your production on the video camera. Make popcorn and watch your original TV production after dinner.

-Mud Pies-

*Getting muddy is always enjoyable for kids. . .
make a pie while you're at it!*

Necessities:
A muddy backyard or garden   Disposable pie pans
Old play clothes

Make mud pies outside. Wear old clothes and "bake" the pies in disposable pie pans. Mom and Dad can tell funny stories about recipes they have messed up in the past while the mud pies are "baking" in the sun. Serve a real pie for dessert after dinner.